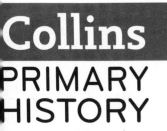

# Collins
## PRIMARY HISTORY

# Changes Within Living

# Living y

## Pupil Book

Sue Temple | Alf Wilkinson

William Collins' dream of knowledge for all began with the publication of his first book in 1819.
A self-educated mill worker, he not only enriched millions of lives, but also founded a flourishing publishing house. Today, staying true to this spirit, Collins books are packed with inspiration, innovation and practical expertise. They place you at the centre of a world of possibility and give you exactly what you need to explore it.

Collins. Freedom to teach.

Published by Collins
An imprint of HarperCollins*Publishers*
The News Building
1 London Bridge Street
London
SE1 9GF

HarperCollins*Publishers*
1st Floor, Watermarque Building,
Ringsend Road, Dublin 4, Ireland

Browse the complete Collins catalogue at
**www.collins.co.uk**

© HarperCollins*Publishers* Limited 2019

Maps © Collins Bartholomew 2019

10 9 8 7 6 5 4

ISBN 978-0-00-831078-3

British Library Cataloguing-in-Publication Data
A catalogue record for this publication is available from the British Library.

Authors: Sue Temple and Alf Wilkinson
Publisher: Lizzie Catford
Product developer: Natasha Paul
Copyeditor: Sally Clifford
Indexer: Jouve India Private Ltd
Proofreader: Nikky Twyman
Image researcher: Alison Prior
Map designer: Gordon MacGilp
Cover designer and illustrator: Steve Evans
Internal designer: EMC Design
Typesetter: Jouve India Private Ltd
Production controller: Rachel Weaver
Printed by Martins the Printers

MIX
Paper from
responsible sources
FSC® C007454

This book is produced from independently certified FSC™ paper to ensure responsible forest management.

For more information visit:
**www.harpercollins.co.uk/green**

The publishers gratefully acknowledge the permission granted to reproduce the copyright material in this book. Every effort has been made to trace copyright holders and to obtain their permission for the use of copyright material. The publishers will gladly receive any information enabling them to rectify any error or omission at the first opportunity.

# Contents

# Introduction

When someone can tell you about their memories of being a child, we call this 'within living memory.' It can be really interesting to find out how life was different for older people when they were children. You can compare their experiences to what your life is like today.

This books explores what different aspects of life were like when your grandparents, or older friends and relatives, were young. It covers living memories of going shopping for food, playing, washing, using technology, going shopping for clothes, going to school, going on holidays and feeling poorly. The experiences in this book are based on what life was like for *some* people, specifically in the United Kingdom. However, you can find out about aspects of life in the past in *your* country by asking *your* older friends and relatives questions. You could ask them about their experiences of the things covered in this book (like shopping or going to school), or you could ask them about anything else that interests you!

It is *very* important to remember that everyone's experiences of life are different. Your older friends and relatives may have very different memories to those explored in this book. Everyone's memories will be different depending on lots of factors, including:

- where in the world they lived
- how much money they had
- what their families were like

... and many more things.

Asking someone questions about what they remember is called **oral history**. This is a sort of enquiry. You should try to record whatever you find out in some way. You could video the conversation, or make a scrap book with photographs and comments. This will become a piece of evidence. You will be able to look at what you found out again. You will also be able to share your findings with other people. You might even notice new things each time you look at your evidence!

Have fun!

# Timeline of events

**1952** The first Disneyland opens

**1938** The first electric home tumble dryer is sold

**1936** Butlin's holiday camp opens in Skegness

**1951** The first supermarket opens in Britain

**1902** The first teddy bear is made

1900   1905   1910   1915   1920   1925   1930   1935   1940   1945   1950

1899 - PAPA'S GREAT GRANDFATHER BORN IN IRELAND

MAMA & PAPA'S GRANDPARENTS BORN

1948 - NANA ROSE BORN

1950 - NANA CHARBOURS

**1936** The first computer is invented

**1947** Oxfam opens its first shop

**1948** The National Health Service starts in the UK

**1949** The first laundrette opens in Britain

**1953** The first Centre Parc opens in Holland

**1955** Polio vaccines are introduced

**1958** Lego is introduced

**1983** The first games console is introduced

**1980** Many people in England own a freezer

**1984** The last record of a child getting polio in the UK

**1977** The first MRI scan of a person happens

**1989** The World Wide Web is started

**1976** Brent Cross, the UK's first out-of-town shopping centre, opens

**1990** 'Nit nurses' disappear

**1969** Comfort, a fabric softener, is introduced

**2002** Smart phones are introduced

1960    1965    1970    1972    1975    1980    1985    1990    1995    2000    2005

PAPA BORN    MAMA BORN    2024 MISHU BORN    2018 KILLELLE BORN

**1970** Most people in England own a fridge

**1995** Tesco and Sainsbury's start online shopping and delivery

**1971** Primary school children stop getting free milk every day in Britain

**1999** Marks and Spencer start selling clothes online

**1986** Corporal punishment stops

**1973** The first mobile phone is invented

**1957** The first BBC schools programmes begin

**1982** The British Government offers to pay half the money for computers in schools

North Pole

GREENLAND

SW

ICELAND

NORWAY

UNITED
KINGDOM DENMAR

IRELAND

GERMAN
AUS
CRC

FRANCE

PORTUGAL

SPAIN

ITA

CANADA

UNITED STATES
OF AMERICA

MOROCCO

ALGERIA

MEXICO

MAURITANIA

MALI

NIGER

CUBA

SENEGAL

JAMAICA

GUINEA

GUATEMALA

NICARAGUA

NIGERIA

COSTA RICA

VENEZUELA

GHANA

PANAMA

GUYANA

ATLANTIC
OCEAN

COLOMBIA

Equator

ECUADOR

GABON

PERU

BRAZIL

PACIFIC
OCEAN

BOLIVIA

PARAGUAY

NA

CHILE

URUGUAY

ARGENTINA

SOUTHERN O

South Pole

ARCTIC OCEAN

RUSSIA

NE

KAZAKHSTAN

MONGOLIA

JAPAN

PACIFIC OCEAN

URKEY

TURKMENISTAN

SYRIA

AFGHANISTAN

CHINA

AEL

IRAQ

IRAN

JORDAN

PAKISTAN

NEPAL

PT

SAUDI ARABIA

OMAN

INDIA

MYANMAR

DAN

ERITREA YEMEN

THAILAND

PHILIPPINES

VIETNAM

UTH DAN

ETHIOPIA

SRI LANKA

SOMALIA

MALAYSIA

KENYA

Equator

INDIAN OCEAN

INDONESIA

PAPUA NEW GUINEA

TANZANIA

SOLOMON ISLANDS

MOZAMBIQUE

VANUATU

MADAGASCAR

AUSTRALIA

NEW ZEALAND

| 1950 | 1960 | 1970 |
|------|------|------|
| 1951 first supermarket | | 1970 most people had fridges |

How often do you or your family go shopping? Do you go every day? Twice a week? Once a week? Once a month? And where do you go shopping? To the market? A small shop? A supermarket? Or out of town? Or do you get your shopping delivered to your home? There are lots of choices.

## Grandma goes shopping

It wasn't always the way it is today. In England, when Grandma was little, most people went shopping every day, to buy milk, bread and other goods that might go off very quickly. It was very difficult to keep food fresh, so people bought little and often. Goods like tea, sugar, flour, butter and even biscuits came in big boxes or cartons and were weighed out and wrapped up for you by the shopkeeper. That meant you could buy very small amounts as you needed them.

## Supermarkets

The first supermarket opened in Britain in 1951 and things slowly began to change. Since then, supermarkets have got bigger and bigger. Also as

*Weighing out sweets in the 1960s*

| 1980 | 1990 | 2000 |
|---|---|---|

1980 many people had freezers

1995 UK supermarkets Tesco and Sainsbury's started online shopping and delivery

more people have got cars, they have often moved out of towns to areas with easy parking. You can even order online and the supermarkets will deliver your shopping right to your door!

▲ *Inside a modern supermarket*

## Fridges

In 1960, very few families had fridges (short for 'refrigerators'), let alone freezers. This changed what people bought. Most food then was bought fresh, or in tins. Fruit (oranges, pears, peaches), vegetables (peas and carrots) and meat (corned beef, for example) were usually bought in tins. Food shops didn't open on Sundays. So Saturday evening, after pay day, was a good time to go shopping, as shopkeepers tried to sell off food that would not keep until Monday.

*1950s refrigerator*

By 1970, over half of families had fridges, so buying food was beginning to change. Food could be kept in the fridge for several days, so you didn't need to go shopping every day. Many more women had jobs and could not shop every day.

## Freezers and microwaves

By the 1980s, many people had a freezer. Frozen food became very popular and many supermarkets had special places in the shop for the big freezers. People began to buy in bulk, and also to buy frozen ready meals, or **convenience foods**. By the 1990s, many families had a microwave oven, which could cook food from frozen in just a few minutes.

*Frozen food aisle in a supermarket*

Some supermarkets opened special stores selling just frozen foods. Frozen foods could be produced anywhere in the world and stored for a very long time. Shopping was changing!

*1984 advert for a microwave*

**Convenience foods:** These are foods which are very easy to prepare — you just pop them in the oven or microwave and cook them. There are no vegetables to peel or chop, and it is easier to wash up afterwards!

### What people were buying

The food people buy has changed too. Many things we buy today were not easy to get hold of in Britain in the 1960s and 1970s. Curries, Chinese food, pizza, pasta and burgers were rarely eaten. Most people ate 'meat and two veg'. Exotic fruits like avocado were unheard of in Britain, yet all these can be widely bought in supermarkets today. Most fruit and vegetables are packaged in plastic instead of being sold loose.

*Avocado – at first, people didn't know what to do with them!*

Fewer foods were imported then, so people ate what was 'in season' (growing at the time). Fresh fruit was plentiful in the autumn, but scarcer and more expensive the rest of the year. Carrots, peas, leeks and parsnips were also more plentiful at some times of the year than others.

# Paying for your shopping

Today, most people use a debit or credit card to pay for much of their shopping. The money is taken automatically out of their bank account. Few people use cash to pay for large amounts any more. In the 1960s, many people didn't even have a bank account – they were paid each week, and they paid for their shopping with cash. Until 1971, there were 240 pennies in a British pound; not 100 as there is today. Prices were given in 'pounds, shillings and pence'.

◀ *Pre-decimal currency*

## Let's think about it!

Ask your parents and grandparents (or older family friends) what shopping was like when they were young. What were the differences between each time? How was each time different to now? What was new when they were young?

Find out what all the different shops were called, and fill in the chart:

| Goods sold | What was the shop called? |
|---|---|
| Cakes and bread | |
| Meat | |
| Fruit and vegetables | |
| Newspapers and magazines | |
| Stamps | |

Did your family and friends tell you about any other shops?

| 1900 | 1910 | 1920 | 1930 | 1940 |
|------|------|------|------|------|

1902 first teddy bear made

Ever since the Stone Age, a long, long time ago, children have been given toys to play with. And many of them would be familiar to us today. The first doll in Britain, for example, was discovered at Stonehenge, and is over 4000 years old!

A

B

## Questions we might ask about old toys

Old toys can tell us a great deal about life in the past. Look carefully at these three pictures of model trains. What is each one made from? Which ones are meant for young children to play with, and which ones are for older children? Which is the oldest? Which is the newest? How can you tell? How do they work?

| 1950 | 1960 | 1970 | 1980 | 1990 |
|------|------|------|------|------|

1958 Lego introduced

1983 first games console introduced

▲ *Three model trains*

## Changing, and staying the same

In some ways toys have stayed the same – each of these is a toy train – but they have also changed. New toys have come along – Lego was first sold in 1958, and Play-Doh in 1956. The first Nintendo game console was in 1983; and the Wii was first sold in 2006.

## Teddy bears

▲ *A teddy bear from the 1930s*

This is a photograph of a teddy from the 1930s. Teddy bears were first made in 1902 and named after the President of the United States, 'Teddy' (or Theodore) Roosevelt, who is said to have refused to shoot a baby bear he found when he was out hunting wild animals. They have been popular toys ever since. How can you tell that this teddy bear is old?

# Similar and different

*A modern teddy bear*

This teddy is new. How is it similar to the teddy in Picture A, and how is it different?

What questions would you like to ask about both of the teddy bears? What could we find out about the past from them? Can you imagine what life must have been like for a child in the 1930s when they played with their teddy bears? Do you think they would have played the same way that you do?

## Outdoor games

Children have always played football and cricket in the street, as well as skipping, marbles, conkers and hopscotch. Most of these games involved little or no equipment and could be played with as many people as were available. It was quite common to play 25-a-side football matches! When houses were small and full of people, and there was less traffic in the road, playing outside was a way to get some fresh air and exercise. How many of these games do children still play outside today? Are there other games you know of that were played outdoors?

*Playing hopscotch*

*A game of cricket in the street*

*Children skipping in the school playground*

## Let's think about it!

Talk to older people about the games they played when they were young. Work out beforehand what questions you want to ask them. Did they play the same kinds of games that you do today? Did they play games without adults around to supervise them?

Did they ever go to the park to play, or to organised play sessions, swimming lessons or other organised sports? How was their childhood play similar to yours? Lots of things have changed, but have any things stayed the same?

What games did they play at school? Are they the same or different to what you play at school?

| 1930 | 1940 | 1950 |
|---|---|---|
| 1933 Dreft, the first washing powder, was introduced | 1938 first electric home tumble dryer sold | 1949 the first laundrette opened in Britain |

## Going to the laundrette

The first **laundrette** opened in Britain in October 1949. By the 1980s, there were over 12,500 of them! Less than half of all homes had a washing machine, because they were very expensive to buy. In October 1949, it cost 2 shillings and 6 pence (12 and a half p) to wash your clothes.

> **Laundrette:**
> This is a shop with lots of electric washing machines in.

## Washing your clothes

The laundrette had really big washing machines. You would load in your clothes, put your money in the slot, and sit and wait for your clothes to be washed. You could, if you had the money, pay extra to use the tumble dryer once your clothes had been washed. Otherwise, you took your wet clothes home with you to dry — either on a washing line outside or on racks in front of the fire in your living room. Some laundrettes had staff who would do your washing for you, but this cost extra money as well.

*A laundrette in the UK*

1960                          1970                          1980

1969 Comfort, a fabric
softener, was introduced

## Who used laundrettes?

Pat Cryer, on her webpage *Join me in the 1900s*, talks of being young and just married, and not being able to afford a washing machine. She used to walk to the local laundrette carrying the dirty clothes in a basket on wheels. She says that you often had to wait to use a dryer, because there weren't as many dryers as washing machines. The weekly trip to the laundrette was a big part of everyday life.

IF you have weekly laundry bills . . .
IF you are feeling the drag of washdays . . .
IF you have a growing family . . .
IF you value your looks and leisure . . .

# It's time you had a
## *Thor*
AUTOMAGIC
WASHING
MACHINE

Thor takes the work literally OFF YOUR HANDS, and washes, rinses and damp dries 8 lbs. of clothes in 30 minutes, costing only ½d. per wash to operate. THOR requires no special plumbing to install— from the day you have it leisure is yours, smooth hands never in water, and a carefree heart . . .
● **Super Agitator for maximum dirt extraction.**
● **Over-flow Rinse — better than any number of separate rinses.**
● **Double Speed Spin Drying.**
✗ *and with the special Dish-Washing Attachment Thor washes-up as well!*
*Easy payments available, Dish-washing Attachment optional*
Write for fullest details to:
Dept. H, Thor Appliances Ltd.
55-59 Oxford Street, London, W.1

*Inside a laundrette in the 1960s*

*1950 advert for a washing machine*

### Monday was wash day...

Before electric washing machines, wash day always started early; sometimes as early as 5 a.m. There would be no time for cooking on wash day; people ate cold leftovers from Sunday. Washing was either done by hand, or using a **copper** if you had one, or a dolly tub. Either way, houses often only had a cold tap so the water had to be heated. Washing had to be separated into white and coloured clothes. Bad stains needed to be soaked overnight before wash day. Most people used bars of soap rather than soap powder, and there were no 'miracle' **biological powders** like today!

**Copper:**
This was a big metal barrel with a fire underneath to wash your clothes in.

**Biological powder:**
This is the washing powder which has special chemicals in it to help get your clothes clean and smelling nice.

◄ *Using a dolly tub to do the washing*

# Drying

Once washed, all the water had to be squeezed out of the washing, using a mangle (see photograph). This was really hard work, and the person using it usually got very wet. Once most of the water was removed, the clothes were hung out to dry. Of course, if it was a wet day, then they would have to be dried indoors, which made the whole house damp and smelly!

*Using a mangle to squeeze out water from the washing*

# Ironing

The dry washing would then need to be folded and ironed before being put away. Few people had electric irons, so they used an old-fashioned iron heated up on the fire. No wonder most women had rough hands – there were no rubber gloves in those days.

*One of the new electric irons that made life much easier – if you could afford one*

25

## Today...

Today, 97 per cent of all homes in the UK have their own washing machines, and often a tumble dryer too. Wash day is no longer restricted to Mondays. People wear more clothes, and need to wash more often. Washing machines can now be programmed to start and finish at any time, often washing overnight using cheaper electricity. Easy-iron programmes cut down lots of the hard work involved in doing the laundry. Wet clothes no longer get spread around the house to dry, and modern washing powders often include nice smells to make clothes seem cleaner and fresher. Wash day is no longer a big chore for most people.

*Modern washing machine and dryer in a utility room,
out of the way and easy to use*

## Let's think about it!

Did your parents help with chores when they were still living at home? What did they have to do? What do you do to help your parents?

Ask your parents if they have any special clothes that cannot be washed in a washing machine. How are they cleaned?

Does your town have a laundrette? If not, find out if it used to have one, and when it closed down.

27

| 1920 | 1930 | 1940 | 1950 | 1960 |
|------|------|------|------|------|

1936 the first computer was invented

## Talking to Granny!

As a present, Granny got a tablet. This makes it much easier to exchange messages with her, as she can contact us wherever she is, not just when she's near her computer. That means we can talk to her more often, and video messaging means that we can see her too, so we know how she is feeling.

Granny with her tablet

## Tim Berners-Lee and the World Wide Web

It has not always been as easy to keep in touch. Until Tim Berners-Lee developed the World Wide Web (www) in 1989, it was difficult for computers to talk to each other — they often spoke different **computer languages**. Once Tim set up the first website in 1991, gradually everyone copied him, and the World Wide Web was born. Keeping in touch with people far away became much easier.

**Computer languages:**
When computers were invented by different people, they all had different languages — like people do. Tim Berners-Lee encouraged everyone to use the same language, to make it much easier for them to communicate.

| 1970 | 1980 | 1990 | 2000 | 2010 |
|------|------|------|------|------|

1973 the first mobile phone was invented

1982 the Government offered to pay half the money for computers in schools, to encourage more people to use them

1989 World Wide Web was started

2002 smart phones introduced

◀ *Tim Berners-Lee at his desk*

## Computers get smaller – and much more powerful

To begin with, computers were enormous, expensive and very slow. Few people could afford them – it was mostly businesses that had computers. Over the last 20 years, all that has changed. Computers are very cheap. It is now possible to have all the memory you need in a tiny tablet. And Granny has bought one.

▲ *A computer from the 1960s*

Public telephone boxes like this were found in every town and village

## Making a phone call

If you wanted to talk to someone, then there was always the telephone – except that, until the 1960s and 1970s, most ordinary people in the UK had to rely on a public call box. It was easy to use a call box if you had a big supply of pennies and the person you wanted to talk to had a phone in their home.

By the 1970s, people were more likely to have a phone in their own home, and it became much easier to keep in touch. The first mobile phone was introduced in 1983 and it was as big as a house brick!

By the 1990s, technology made mobile phones cheaper and more reliable to use, so the personal mobile phone was born. By the mid-2000s, nearly everyone in the UK – young and old, rich and poor – had a mobile phone. The first **smart phone** was introduced in 2002, and within 10 years they became cheap enough to become very popular, combining telephones, cameras and computers. Some phones today have more power and memory than computers used to!

**Smart phones:**
These are mobile phones which can connect to the internet.

*An old mobile phone*

*A modern smart phone*

A postbox in London. Notice the EIIR on the postbox, telling us that this postbox was put up while Elizabeth II was queen

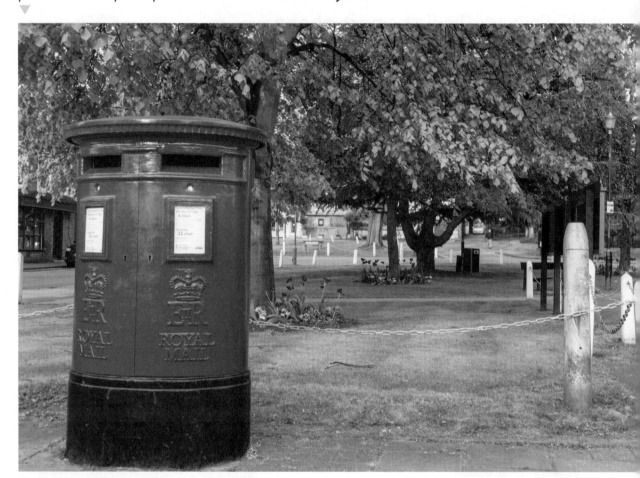

## When Granny was young

When Granny was young, the main way she communicated was by post. In the UK, in 1965, it cost 4d (less than 2p) to send a letter. Before 1971, money was in pounds, shillings and pence. By 1980, it cost 10p, and by the year 2000 you would have to pay 19p to send a letter.

Letters were posted in the postbox and the postal worker would collect it and deliver it in a day or two. People sometimes wrote to friends and family every week. It all took a long time. But it was the only way to keep in touch if you didn't live close to your family and friends.

## Greetings cards

Most people sent greetings cards through the post, and it was usual to send a postcard to friends and relatives whenever you went on holiday. This showed you were thinking about them, and let them know what you were up to. Millions of postcards and greetings cards were delivered by postal workers every year.

*A holiday postcard from the 1960s*

## Let's think about it!

Find out how many things in your home are controlled by a computer – there will probably be quite a few!

| 1940 | 1950 | 1960 |
|------|------|------|

1947 Oxfam, a charity which fights poverty, opened its first shop

▲ *Waiting for a bus in the rain*

## Getting a new coat

When some people were young in the 1960s, they were very lucky. If you were the oldest in your family, you often got the new coat and, when you grew too big for it, it was handed down to your younger

70                    1980                         1990                    2000

1976 Brent Cross, the UKs first
out-of-town shopping centre, opened

1999 Marks and Spencer
started selling clothes online

brothers or sisters. Some adults
were very good at sewing, so
could take apart an adult's coat
and make one for a child from
the cloth. It was difficult to buy
new coats for children with not
much money.

## The Clothing Club

Sometimes, the only way to get
a new coat in the UK was by using

*Ready for the new school year, 1960s style*

the Clothing Club. Parents would pay in a little money each week, until
there was enough to buy a coat; or, perhaps, they would buy the coat
from the Clothing Club – usually paying a little bit more for it – and pay
back the cost of the coat every week until they had paid it all off.
Then they could buy another coat for another child.

The start of the new school year was especially expensive for parents!
The club was a way to spread the cost of new clothes over many weeks.
Some parents never managed to pay back all the money they
had borrowed.

### Buying a coat today

There have never been so many different places to buy a coat as there are today. You can buy online and have it delivered to your home the very next day. There are shops on the high street, and out-of-town shopping centres. There are chain stores, supermarkets, factory outlets and individual shops. You can have almost any style, size or colour you want. Sometimes there is just too much choice.

▲

*Buying clothes has never been so easy*

*A charity shop in Hove, UK*

## Secondhand clothes

Most high streets in the UK now have several charity shops. These take your unwanted items and sell them to raise funds for the charity. Lots of people like to browse there, to see what they can find. If you don't have much money, then this might be the only place you can afford to shop. Lots of people, however, like to shop in charity shops, looking for a bargain, or something they might not be able to afford otherwise. It also makes them feel good that their money is helping to support a charity.

In the 1960s and 1970s, most people would only have one outdoor coat. Today it is quite common to have winter coats, summer coats, raincoats, warm coats, dry coats, ski coats, and more.

37

### Tailor-made?

Perhaps the best way to get a new coat that fits well is to get it made to measure by a **tailor**. Throughout history, people who could afford it have had their clothes made especially to fit them. This involves a lot of measuring, deciding the style, choosing the fabric, the lining, the buttons...
It is a very individual way to buy a coat.

**Tailor:**
Someone who makes clothing to fit you.

*A made-to-measure tailor in a shop in Savile Row, London*

Traditionally, most made-to-measure tailors worked in Savile Row, in London, and rich people would go to London once or twice a year to be measured for a coat and new clothes. Nowadays, people living in the UK can be measured in their own home, and their coat is made by a tailor living in China or India and posted to them.

*Order online, send your measurements to China, and receive your coat in the UK by airmail within three weeks!*

## Let's think about it!

Ask your parents and older relatives what happened when they were children. Did they get a brand-new coat, or a 'hand-me-down'?

Measure someone in your class for new clothes.

Visit a local shop that sells secondhand goods. What kinds of things do they sell?

1957 first BBC schools programmes began

1971 the free milk for all primary children every day stopped

## Schools then and now

*A village school, 1957*

Imagine what it would be like going to school in this village school in 1957. What are the buildings like? How big is the school? What play equipment is there? How secure is the site? How is the school heated?

| 1980 | 1990 | 2000 |
|------|------|------|

1986 corporal punishment was stopped

1990 by now, 'nit nurses' had disappeared

*Hinguar Community Primary School, in Essex, UK, built in 2012*

Imagine what it would be like going to school in this school today. What are the buildings like? Think about your school. How big is the school? What play equipment is there outside? How secure is the site? How is the school heated?

## Comparing then and now

Look carefully at the two pictures of the outside of primary schools – one from 1957 and one from 2012. We can learn a lot about going to school from the buildings. What would it be like to go to school in each of these buildings? Which one would you prefer to go to school in, and why?

## Inside the classroom

*Inside a classroom, 1960s*

Now look carefully at the photograph of a classroom in the 1960s. What can you *see*? How is the classroom *similar* to the one you are sitting in, and how is it *different*? Make a list of all the similarities, and all the differences, you can find.

What kind of lessons do you think would take place in a classroom like this? How can you tell?

# What children would learn at school

Since 1870, everyone in the UK has had to go to school from the age of 5. Nowadays, children can also attend preschool before that. At first, people thought it was important for children to go to school and learn how to read, write and add up. They were also taught about religion. Gradually, more and more subjects were added to the curriculum, including science, history, geography and PE.

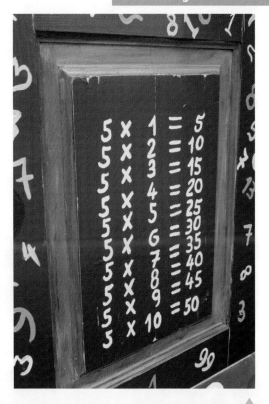

Posters like this one, showing the 5 times table, would be on every classroom wall

Teachers were very strict. If you misbehaved, you would be beaten – sometimes with a cane, sometimes with a strap. This was called **corporal punishment**. You would be expected to listen, not talk, and learn by rote – listening to the teacher and repeating what he or she said. You had to learn your times tables off by heart, and even be expected to recite long poems from memory!

**Corporal punishment:** This was when a teacher hit a child with a strap or stick to punish them for doing something bad.

Nearly everyone walked to school, often several kilometres – and they might walk home again for lunch. It was a good way to keep fit. Classes were often large – some classes had 50 children in them. Nearly every school offered swimming lessons, but they were usually in a very cold outdoor pool.

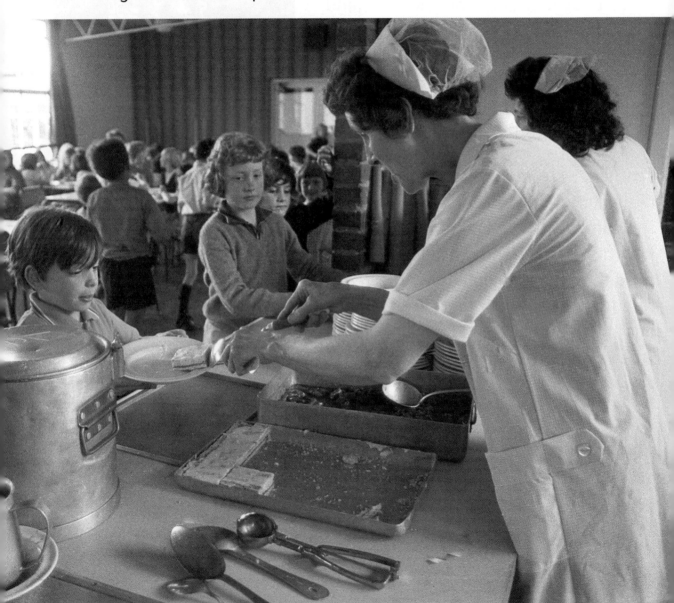

*School meals, 1960s style*

Every term there would be a visit from the 'nit nurse', who would very carefully check your hair to make sure you didn't have any headlice. Toilets were usually outdoors, at the bottom of the yard, making them very cold and isolated in the winter. Children tried not to go to the toilet while at school, and would wait until home time instead! Every child had a small bottle of milk at school every day. Milk is good for growing children, so this was to make pupils stronger and healthier.

*Children sitting on the floor in the school hall, 1967*

## Changes...

Some things were changing. During the 1960s, the School Broadcasting Council started making radio programmes for schools. Children would often sit on the floor in the hall and listen to the programmes. By the end of the 1960s, some schools even had televisions.

### Let's think about it!

Make a table showing the differences between school now, and when your parents were there. Talk to your friends about the differences.

Make another table showing what school was like for your grandparents. Was it different to your parents' school? What has changed from then to now? What has stayed the same?

1930 | 1940

1936 Butlin's holiday camp opened in Skegness

## We're all going on a summer holiday...

Going on holiday is one of the things we look forward to the most. Packing... Loading the car... Setting off... Perhaps surprisingly, 75 per cent of British people still take their holidays in the UK in 2019. There are lots of places to choose from – seaside or mountains; town or countryside. And there are also plenty of places to stay – campsites, caravan parks, holiday camps, hotels, apartments or cottages. You can even stay in a castle if you want to, and if you can afford it!

*One of many beaches in the UK*

1952 the first
Disneyland opened

1950                                                                                    1960

1952 the first package
holidays to sunny places
abroad started

1953 the first Centre
Parc opened in
Holland

## Going abroad

Many people choose to go abroad for their holidays. Today, it is easy
for people who live in the UK to fly to Spain, Greece, Portugal or
Turkey for a 'package' holiday – a holiday that includes travel, hotel or
apartment, even all food and drink if you wish. Throughout the summer,
planes fly from airports across the country to places around the world,
taking holidaymakers looking for sunshine and relaxation.

More people in Britain are having more than one holiday a year.
Some are in Britain and some abroad – or even further away in places
like Africa or the West Indies, for winter sun as well as summer sun!
People have more holidays now than they used to.

*Planes waiting for their passengers*
▼

## Holidays in the 1960s

It wasn't always like this. In the 1960s, it was quite common for workers in the UK to have only two weeks' holiday a year. The whole town might shut down for a week while all the factories and their workers went on holiday at the same time. As most people didn't have cars, people used the train or buses. They usually went to the seaside and stayed in a **boarding house** or a caravan. Seaside towns such as Blackpool, Skegness and Great Yarmouth were all very popular places to go. If you couldn't afford to go away, you might go out for day trips specially organised by local coach firms.

**Boarding house:**
This was like a small hotel which did bed and breakfast. You weren't allowed in the house during the day – only to sleep and have your breakfast!

◀ 1960s photo of Blackpool and its famous tower

## Staying in a caravan

Caravans were much smaller than they are today. Quite often there was only one bedroom, and children slept on 'pull-down' beds made from the seats and/or table! There might be a cold tap, or you might have to carry water from a pipe next to the toilet block. Caravans didn't have their own showers and toilets – you had to walk across the field to the ones everyone shared! Yet people still enjoyed their week – or two – of fresh air by the sea or in the countryside.

*Donkey rides on the beach*

*1960s caravan park in Dorset*

## Holiday camps

An alternative to caravans or camping was going to spend a week at a holiday camp, like Butlin's or Pontins. You could stay in a chalet. This had a little more space. Meals were provided in huge dining rooms, where hundreds of people were fed at the same time. You had to make sure you went to the right sitting or you missed your meal!

## Entertainment

There were all kinds of entertainments, both day and night, including indoor amusements in case it rained. Top entertainers would perform in the ballroom some evenings, and there were all kinds of competitions, from 'Glamorous Granny' to snooker and darts. There was something to do every minute of the day, from breakfast at 8 a.m. until midnight!

## Theme parks

During the 1970s and 1980s theme parks, like Alton Towers

*An advert for a Butlin's holiday camp chalet, 1960s*

*Roller coaster at a modern theme park*

and Drayton Manor Theme Park, became popular places to go for a day out in the UK. New-style holiday resorts, like Center Parcs, appeared. Here you could cycle, walk or swim and have a 'healthy' holiday in attractive surroundings. Resorts and places to stay have had to keep updating themselves to continue to attract people who want to have fun on holiday.

*A 'glamping' pod*

One of the latest trends is '**glamping**' – camping in a little bit more luxury, with beds, bed linen, heating and cooking facilities provided. Things have certainly changed since the 1960s!

**Glamping:**
This is a short way to say 'glamorous camping' – everything is more luxurious when you are glamping, as you have a proper bed, heating and private bathroom.

## Let's think about it!

Make a graph or chart showing all the different places everyone in your class went on holiday last year. How many people went in an aeroplane for their holiday?

Talk to your parents about the kinds of holidays they had when they were children. What kinds of things did they do when they were on holiday? What is the same, and what is different, between then and now?

Some people think glamping only started recently. See if you can find out about glamping in the past.

| 1940 | 1950 | 1960 | 1970 |
|---|---|---|---|

1948 the National Health Service started in the UK

1955 polio vaccinations were introduced

## Going to the doctor

What happens when you feel unwell? What do your parents do? Perhaps they look in the medicine cabinet for their 'special bottle' of medicine. Every family seems to have one. It cures colds, headaches, aches and pains...

**Pharmacy:**
Also known in Britain as a chemist. This is where you go to get medicines and tablets to make you better when you are ill.

*A visit to the **pharmacy** for advice and to buy medicines*

| 1980 | 1990 | 2000 | 2010 |
|------|------|------|------|

1977 the first
MRI scan of a
person

1984 the last record
of a child getting
polio in the UK

Parents might go to the supermarket to buy medicine if they think they know what is wrong with you, or they might go to the pharmacy to ask for advice. Or they might make an appointment with the family doctor. Nearly everyone in the UK has a family doctor. You can usually get to see the doctor in a day or two.

*A doctor talking to a patient*

The doctor will look at you carefully, listen to your breathing and perhaps take some blood for tests. They might give you medicines. If they are not sure what is wrong with you, they will send you to see a specialist at a local hospital. There, you could have an X-ray or MRI scan to find out what is wrong. Finally, you will be treated and get well.

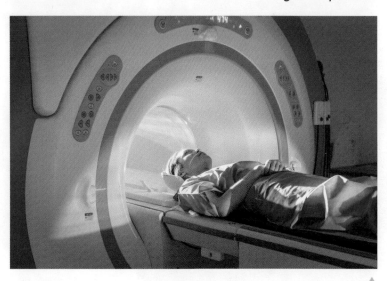

*Having an MRI scan at hospital*

### It wasn't always like this

In 1948, the National Health Service (NHS) was set up in Britain. Everyone could now have free access to doctors, dentists and opticians. Before then, to visit a doctor, people had to pay. Most people couldn't afford to pay and so didn't go to the doctor unless it was a real emergency. People relied on neighbours and friends who could help make them better.

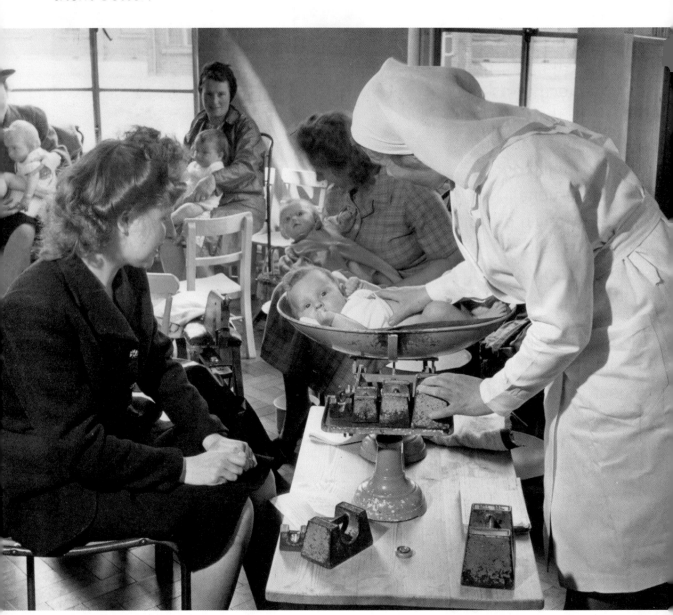

*Children's health clinic, 1948, where mums and children were seen every month*

## Child deaths

One of the biggest changes in Britain since the 1960s has been the huge fall in the number of babies and young children that die. Before the 1960s, many young children died of measles, polio, diphtheria, or other 'children's illnesses'. During the 1960s, the British government introduced **vaccinations** against these diseases for everyone under 15, and deaths from them virtually disappeared. Nowadays very few babies and young children die.

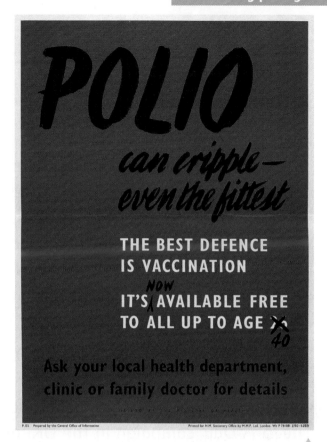

1960s poster encouraging people to have the polio vaccine

## New hospitals

Since the 1960s, many new hospitals have been built, and some old ones updated. Every town was to have its own district hospital where local doctors could send their patients. Can you find out when your local hospital was built? Many more doctors and nurses were employed to look after the patients.

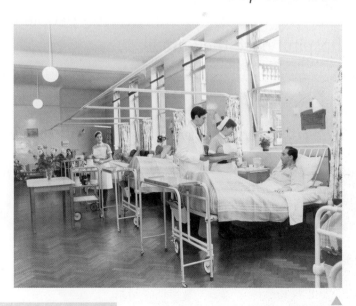

Hospital ward in the 1960s

**Vaccinations:** These are injections which contain special medicine to help make sure you don't catch some diseases.

### Killer diseases

People today live longer than in the past, although there are new, different, killer diseases. Cancer, heart disease, liver disease and dementia are some new major causes of death. Some doctors argue these are what are called 'lifestyle' diseases. They are caused by the way we live. People eat too much, eat too many fatty or sugary foods, don't take enough exercise, and spend too long sitting in front of the television or computer. In 2015, almost half of men and women in Britain were **obese** or overweight.

### Prevention or cure?

Governments are putting a lot of effort into trying to prevent diseases. The '5 A Day' campaign in the UK, getting people to eat five portions of fruit and vegetables daily, is a perfect example. 'Couch to 5K' is another one, encouraging people to run every day. They argue it is cheaper in the long run to change the way people live rather than treat them in hospital once they are ill.

*The UK government encourages people to eat more fruit and vegetables*
▼

# In hospital

In the last 30 years, medicine has changed a great deal. There are many new treatments. People can have their organs replaced, or artificial hips or knees to replace damaged ones. Laser and **keyhole surgery** make operations easier. New medicines treat illnesses. Doctors understand better how the human body works. But is it very expensive. Some people wonder if we can continue to spend so much money on treating people in hospital.

**Keyhole surgery:** This is where the surgeon makes a tiny cut to do something inside your body to make you better.

*A children's ward in a UK hospital*

## Let's think about it!

Ask a nurse from the local hospital to come and talk to your class, or go and visit a local doctor's surgery. What is it like to be ill now? How has that changed?

Find out when your local hospital was built. Compare it to photographs of a hospital in the 1960s. What is the same? What is different? What are the nurses wearing? Why has that changed?

# Combined Lower Primary History timeline

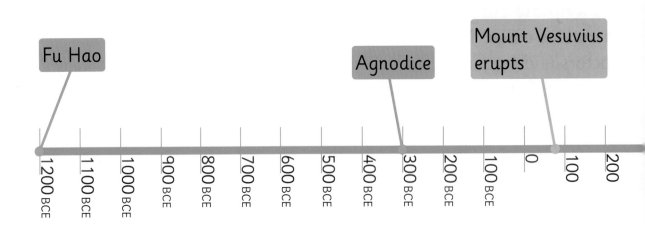

Fu Hao

Agnodice

Mount Vesuvius erupts

1200 BCE
1100 BCE
1000 BCE
900 BCE
800 BCE
700 BCE
600 BCE
500 BCE
400 BCE
300 BCE
200 BCE
100 BCE
0
100
200

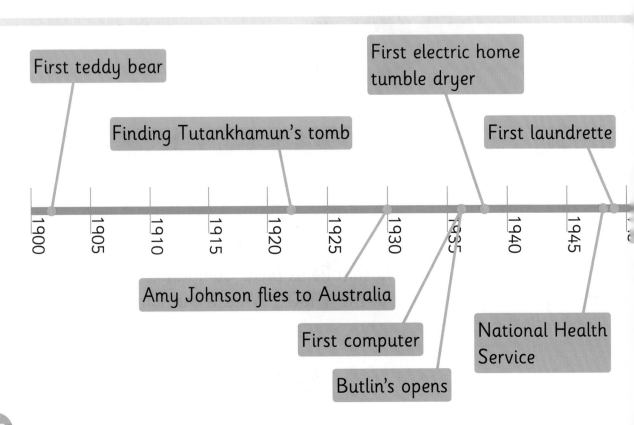

First teddy bear

Finding Tutankhamun's tomb

First electric home tumble dryer

First laundrette

1900
1905
1910
1915
1920
1925
1930
1935
1940
1945

Amy Johnson flies to Australia

First computer

National Health Service

Butlin's opens

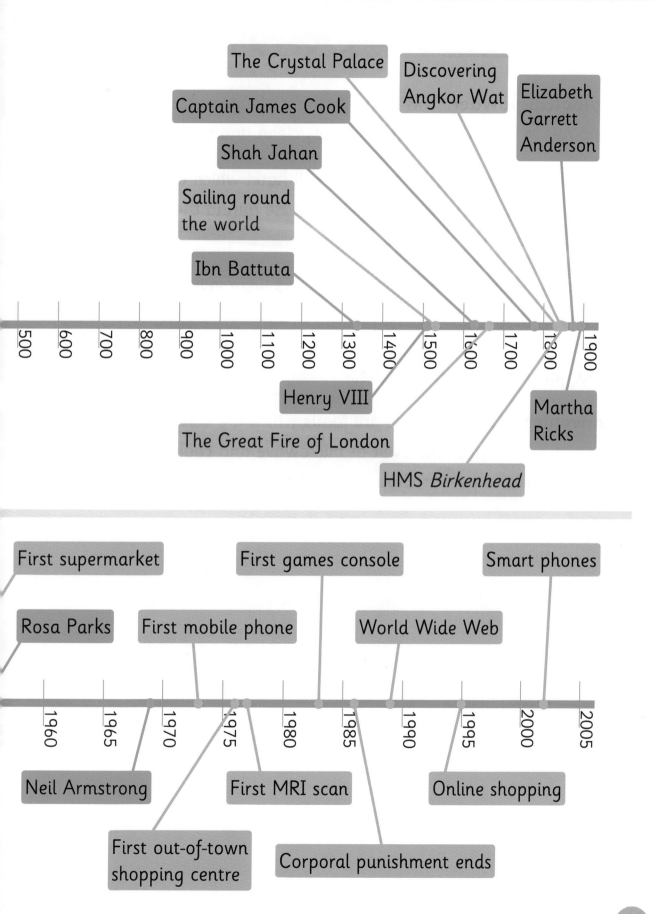

The Crystal Palace

Discovering Angkor Wat

Elizabeth Garrett Anderson

Captain James Cook

Shah Jahan

Sailing round the world

Ibn Battuta

500 600 700 800 900 1000 1100 1200 1300 1400 1500 1600 1700 1800 1900

Henry VIII

The Great Fire of London

Martha Ricks

HMS *Birkenhead*

First supermarket

First games console

Smart phones

Rosa Parks

First mobile phone

World Wide Web

1960 1965 1970 1975 1980 1985 1990 1995 2000 2005

Neil Armstrong

First MRI scan

Online shopping

First out-of-town shopping centre

Corporal punishment ends

# Glossary

**Biological powder:** This is the washing powder which has special chemicals in it to help get your clothes clean and smelling nice.

**Boarding house:** This was like a small hotel which did bed and breakfast. You weren't allowed in the house during the day – only to sleep and have your breakfast!

**Computer languages:** When computers were invented by different people, they all had different languages – like people do. Tim Berners-Lee encouraged everyone to use the same language, to make it much easier for them to communicate.

**Convenience foods:** These are foods which are very easy to prepare – you just pop them in the oven or microwave and cook them. There are no vegetables to peel or chop, and it is easier to wash up afterwards!

**Copper:** This was a big metal barrel with a fire underneath to wash your clothes in.

**Corporal punishment:** This was when a teacher hit a child with a strap or stick to punish them for doing something bad.

**Glamping:** This is a short way to say 'glamorous camping' – everything is more luxurious when you are glamping, as you have a proper bed, heating and private bathroom.

**Keyhole surgery:** This is where the surgeon makes a tiny cut to do something inside your body to make you better.

**Laundrette:** This is a shop with lots of electric washing machines in.

**Pharmacy:** Also known in Britain as a chemist. This is where you go to get medicines and tablets to make you better when you are ill.

**Smart phones:** These are mobile phones which can connect to the internet.

**Tailor:** Someone who makes clothing to fit you.

**Vaccinations:** These are injections which contain special medicine to help make sure you don't catch some diseases.

# Index

# Acknowledgements

The publishers wish to thank the following for permission to reproduce images. Every effort has been made to trace copyright holders and to obtain their permission for the use of copyright materials. The publishers will gladly receive any information enabling them to rectify any error or omission at the first opportunity.

(t = top, c = centre, b = bottom, r = right, l = left)

p5 India Picture/Shutterstock; p10 The Photolibrary Wales/Alamy Stock Photo; p11 Gorodenkoff/Shutterstock; p12 H. Armstrong Roberts/ClassicStock/Getty Images; p13t MM Stock/Shutterstock; p13b Image Courtesy of The Advertising Archives; p14 FabrikaSimf/Shutterstock; p15 Ivan Vdovin/Alamy Stock Photo; p16 Jakub Krechowicz/Alamy Stock Photo; pp16-17 Ciprian Gherghias/Alamy Stock Photo; p17 D. Hurst/Alamy Stock Photo; p18 Dorling Kindersley ltd/Alamy Stock Photo; p19 Jesus Cervantes/Shutterstock; p20t NadyaEugene/Shutterstock; p20b Trinity Mirror/Mirrorpix/Alamy Stock Photo; p21 roger askew/Alamy Stock Photo; p22 Fotomatador./Alamy Stock Photo; p23b Flo Smith/Alamy Stock Photo; p23t Hera Vintage Ads/Alamy Stock Photo; p24 Chronicle/Alamy Stock Photo; p25t INTERFOTO/Alamy Stock Photo; p25b Granger Historical Picture Archive/Alamy Stock Photo; p26 Evgeny Atamanenko/Shutterstock; p27 Alex Segre/Alamy Stock Photo; p28 Odua Images/Shutterstock; p29t CERN/ SCIENCE PHOTO LIBRARY; p29b ClassicStock/Alamy Stock Photo; p30 globetrotters/Shutterstock; p31l Roman Vukolov/Alamy Stock Photo; p31r Es sarawuth/Shutterstock; p32 john mobbs/Shutterstock; p33 David Scott/Alamy Stock Photo; p34 Allan Cash Picture Library/Alamy Stock Photo; p35 Martyn Evans/Alamy Stock Photo; p36 Pavel L Photo and Video/Shutterstock; p37 Roger Utting/ Shutterstock; p38 Roger Hutchings/Alamy Stock Photo; p39 robertharding/Alamy Stock Photo; p40 Trinity Mirror/Mirrorpix/Alamy Stock Photo; p41 Justin Kase z12z/Alamy Stock Photo; p42 Black Country Images/Alamy Stock Photo; p43 Keith Douglas/Alamy Stock Photo; p44 Allan Cash Picture Library/Alamy Stock Photo; p45 Allan Cash Picture Library/Alamy Stock Photo; p46 Jaroslaw Kilian/Shutterstock; p47 bibiphoto/Shutterstock; p48 Chronicle/Alamy Stock Photo; p49b Paul Collis/Alamy Stock Photo; p49t lynn hilton/Alamy Stock Photo; p50t Amoret Tanner/Alamy Stock Photo; p50b Doug Lemke/Shutterstock; p51 Mick Harper/Shutterstock; p52 wavebreakmedia/Shutterstock; p53t Monkey Business Images/Shutterstock; p53b Monty Rakusen/Alamy Stock Photo; p54 Popperfoto/Getty Images; p55t Wellcome Library, London; p55b George Freston/Stringer/Getty Images; p56 Richard Pinder/ Shutterstock; p57 JOHN KELLERMAN/Alamy Stock Photo.